Why is Australia often referred to as being "down under"?

World Book
answers YOUR questions
- about -
people and places

WORLD
BOOK

www.worldbook.com

The questions in this book came from curious kids just like you who want to make sense of the world. They wrote to us at World Book with nothing but a question and a dream that the question they've agonized over would finally be answered.

Some questions made us laugh. Others made us cry. And a few made us question absolutely everything we've ever known. No matter the responses they induced, all the questions were good questions.

There isn't a strict rule for what makes a question good. But asking any question means that you want to learn and to understand. And both of those things are very good.

Adults are always asking, "What did you learn at school today?" Instead, we think they should be asking, **"Did you ask a good question today?"**

Where does Paris get its name?

From a little shop on the Rue Mouffetard.

Just kidding! That's the name of a street in Paris. The city was named "Paris" about two thousand years ago—way before the Eiffel Tower or any delicious pastry shops. In ancient times, a Celtic tribe called the Parisii lived in what is now Paris. The Parisii occupied an island, called Île de la Cité, in the Seine River. It is not far from the Rue Mouffetard.

Did George Washington Carver invent peanut butter?

No.
But he created many things with peanuts—over 300, in fact.

He made a milk substitute, face powder, printer's ink, and soap. George Washington Carver and inventions go together like, well, peanut butter and jelly.

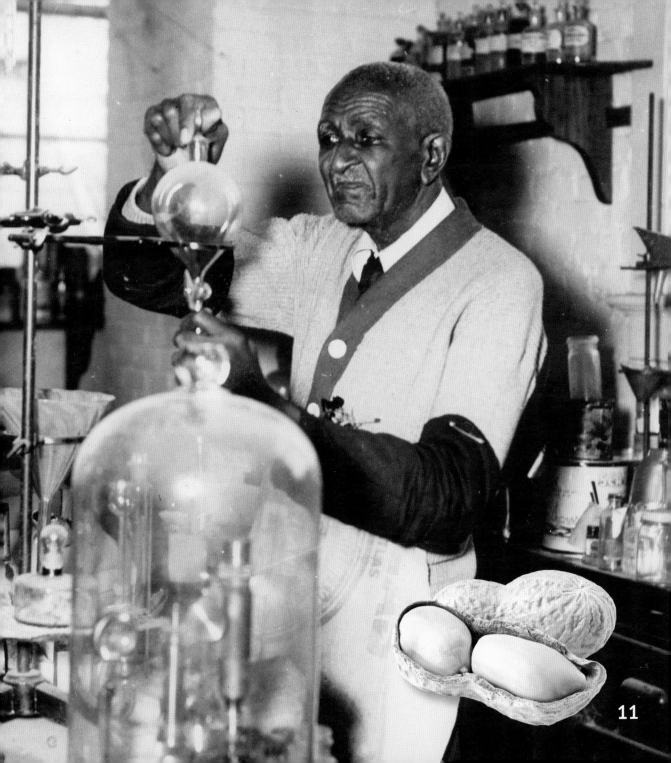

What does the U.S. Supreme Court do for a living?

Think critically.

That sounds nice, doesn't it? But it's a lot—and we mean *a lot*—of critical thinking. The Supreme Court thinks critically to decide if a law follows rules written in the Constitution of the United States. Once the Court makes its decision, all the other courts in the United States follow it. Sometimes people think the Supreme Court didn't do enough critical thinking. Then the process starts all over again.

What is an economy?

Something adults stress out about.

An economy is a very complex concept. It is made up of people, money, and work. People play different roles in an economy. There are buyers and sellers, businesses and employees, and governments. They all work together to determine how many and what types of goods and services everyone wants. They also figure out how to produce these things and how to provide them to people. Who knew you were part of an economy?

When did the samurai first start?

Way, way, way back when.

Samurai were members of the warrior class in Japan. The warrior tradition of customs and values was handed down over many generations. The samurais defended the estates of the nobles. The samurai tradition began about one thousand years ago. They would value your talent riding a horse, your skill with the bow, your strong discipline, and your bravery.

How was written language created?

It all started with emojis—in a way.

Written language probably began with pictograms. They were simple drawings used for communication. It's kind of like when you text a picture of a smiley face with its tongue out when you are hungry. Or a frustrated not-so-smiley face when you're hangry. The pictograms became more complex until they formed logograms. Those were symbols that stood for the words in a language. The Sumerians found that they could use symbols of objects that were easy to picture to stand for words that sounded similar but were hard to picture. That's called *phonetization*. People began to use the system to write about all sorts of things.

When did the
Model T
Ford
come out?

1908

Before that time, you didn't see a lot of cars on the street. And, if you did, a wealthy man with a huge mustache, monocle—and whatever other things really wealthy people wore back then—was probably driving it. Henry Ford changed this. He made the Model T using an assembly line. This meant that the car could be sold at a better price to more Americans. The Model T was probably the most historically important car ever produced.

What is the largest country in the world?

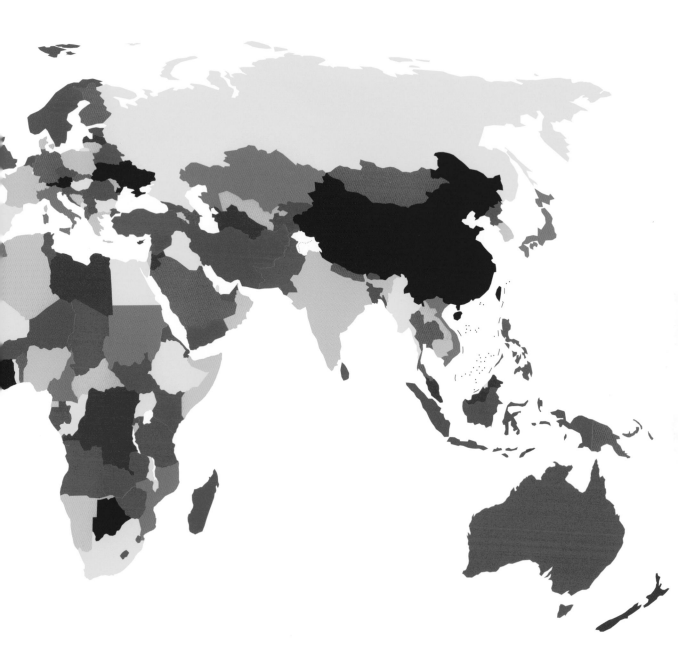

Russia.

It covers 6,601,670 square miles (17,098,246 square kilometers). The smallest country in the world is Vatican City. It is 0.17 square miles (0.44 square kilometer). Russia could fit many Vatican Cities in its boundaries.

Russia

35

Is the Code of Hammurabi fair or unfair?

37

Depends on who you ask.

The Code of Hammurabi was a set of laws that King Hammurabi ordered to be written down. He ruled Babylon from 1792 to 1750 B.C. The code covers a lot of things: family laws, trade, loans, debts, and witchcraft. Sometimes the guilty person had their tongue, hands, eyes, or ears removed. The punishments were not always equal, though. Social status often determined the punishment.

39

Was there a real Lion King?

In a way. But he wasn't named Simba. Sundiata Keita *(sun JAHT ah KAY tah)* founded the Mali Empire in West Africa in 1235. He ruled until about 1260. He made the Mali Empire into one of the largest and wealthiest of Africa's ancient

empires. He also overthrew an evil king and united all the people around him. Simba's character is based on Sundiata's bravery and achievements.

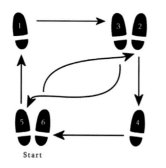

Why do people dance?

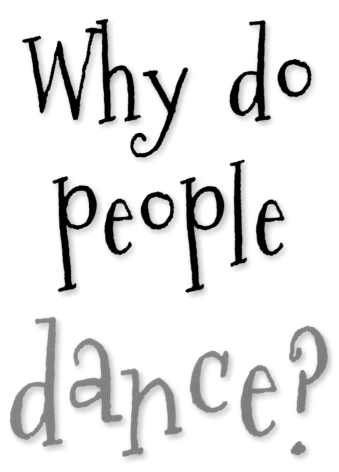

For as many reasons as there are rules in ballroom dancing— and there are a lot.

Dance is an art form and a social activity. It is a type of communication and form of recreation. The great thing is that anyone can dance. You just have to move to the rhythm.

Who is Marie Curie?

49

Marie Curie was a scientist who studied matter, energy, and chemicals.

She was the first woman awarded a Nobel Prize—and a second one! She discovered the chemical elements radium and polonium. That means you have her to thank whenever you see an x ray of your busted-up leg. That x ray is the first step in getting you **cure**-ied.

Why did Egyptians mummify their dead?

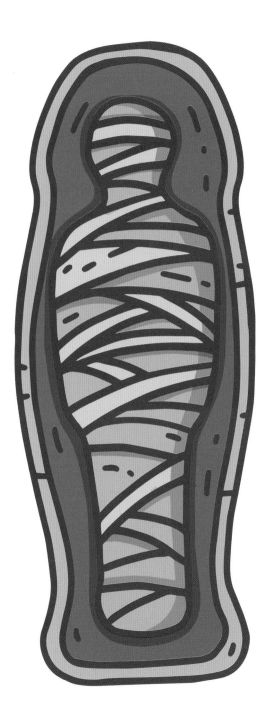

53

Because daddifying wasn't properly preserving the bodies of the dead. And that's the whole point. Egyptians mummified their dead to preserve them for the next life. To *mummify* means to preserve and to dry.

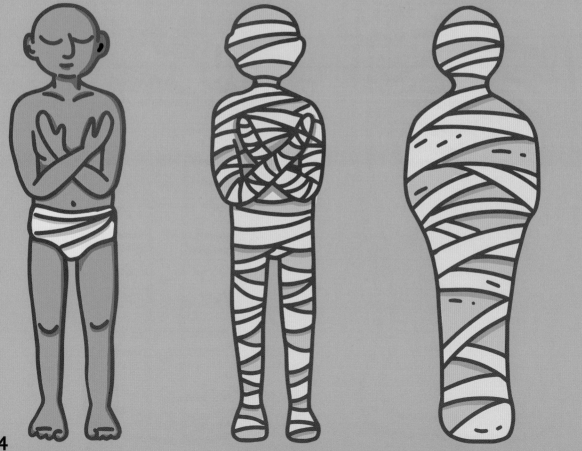

his prevented the corpse from decaying. A body was
rapped in layers of linen strips and put in a coffin. Then
he mummy was put in a tomb. Sometimes a corpse had
ompany—Egyptians mummified cats and monkey, too.
everal Egyptian mummies have lasted to the present day.

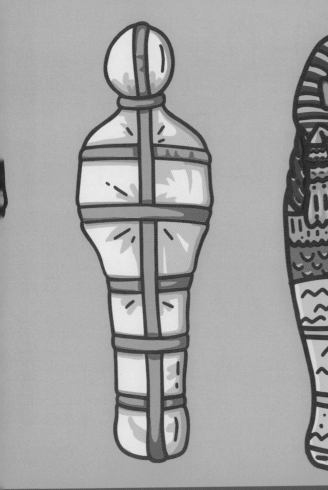

Why is the Leaning Tower of Pisa *leaning?*

The architect who did not get the job got *really* upset one day.

He was walking to his office to work on another, less-awesome tower and just punched it. We're joking! It was much less dramatic. The tower was built on soft ground. The ground was made of clay, fine sand, and shells. Three stories into the construction, the builders realized the tower didn't have a strong foundation. Scientists predict that the Tower will be stable for a few hundred more years. Well, unless the ghost of the grudge-holding architect returns...

When did JAZZ begin?

And a one, a two, a one, two, three, four. You could tell the beginning of this explanation thanks to the clever jazz-related opening. Telling the beginning of jazz, though, is much more difficult. The *history* of jazz began in the late 1800's. The music came from black American music, African rhythms, American band traditions and instruments, and European harmonies and forms. These came together to create a genre of music that is the cat's pajamas! That's Jazz for "Great." To know that, you have to be hip to the jive.

Why was the Great

Wall of China built?

To protect China against enemies. The wall was built over many centuries. But the Ming Dynasty is known for the wall. In response to Mongol attacks, the Ming government started building a major wall in the late 1400's. This wall included most of what remains today. Did you know that you can't actually see the Great Wall from the moon? That news isn't so great, because it would be really great if you could.

When is the Olympic flame put out?

After all the Olympians have huffed and puffed on it.

It's exhausting to deliver a perfect gymnastics routine. But that's definitely not the case because the flame would be blown out after the very first event. The Olympic flame is put out at the Closing Ceremony, after hundreds of premier athletes have huffed and puffed and cried and celebrated.

Did the Underground Railroad

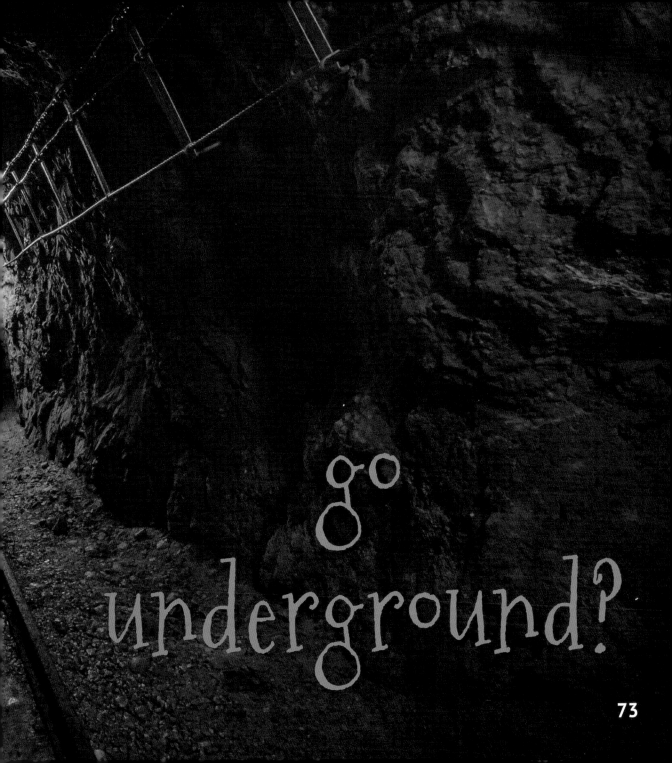

go
underground?

It did not.

The Underground Railroad was an informal system that helped slaves in the southern United States. They were trying to escape to the northern United States, Canada, and other places that prohibited slavery. The system was called the Underground Railroad because of the swift and secret way in which slaves escaped.

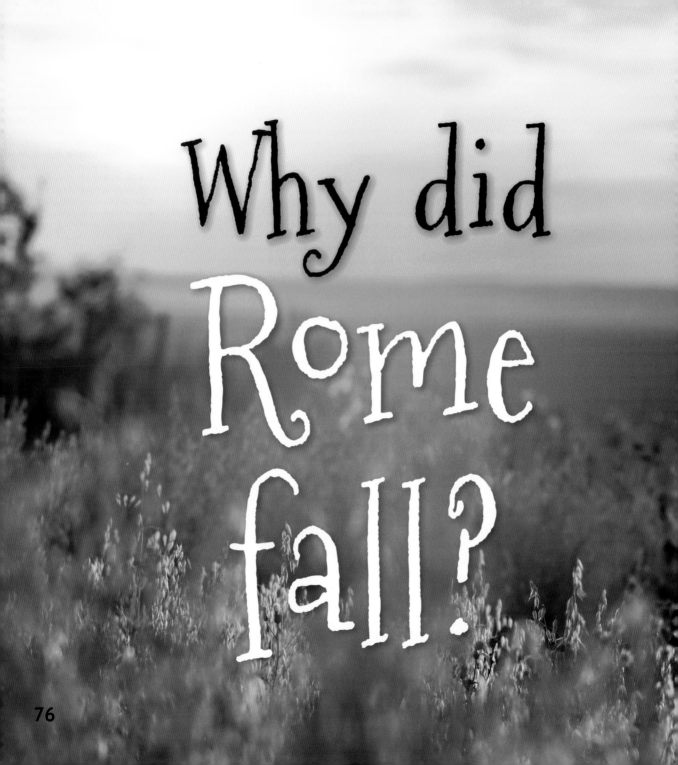

Why did Rome fall?

The Roman Empire was enormously powerful.

In the A.D. 100's and 200's, it governed about half of Europe, much of the Middle East, and the north coast of Africa. That is a *lot* to govern. Ultimately, it was the reason for its downfall. The empire was too much to govern. If you're thinking, "I bet it was that jealous architect in Pisa," you're wrong—the incidents were centuries apart.

Where do the finest rubies come from?

From the finest stores.

There, they are stored in the finest
safes made by the finest locksmiths this
fine world has ever seen. Before that,
they come from Myanmar, a country in
southeast Asia. The African countries
Kenya, Tanzania, and Madagascar are also
producers of the finest rubies. Maybe
you, all your friends, and every kid in
your whole school could pool your lunch
money to buy some of the finest rubies.

Who was Confucius, and when did he live?

"You cannot open a book without learning something."
—Confucius

Confucius was an incredibly influential philosopher—maybe even the *most* influential—in Chinese history. No one knows the exact years he lived. It was most likely between 551 and 479 B.C. His ideas are called *Confucianism*. He believed it was very important to develop strong character and responsibility. How can you strengthen your character?

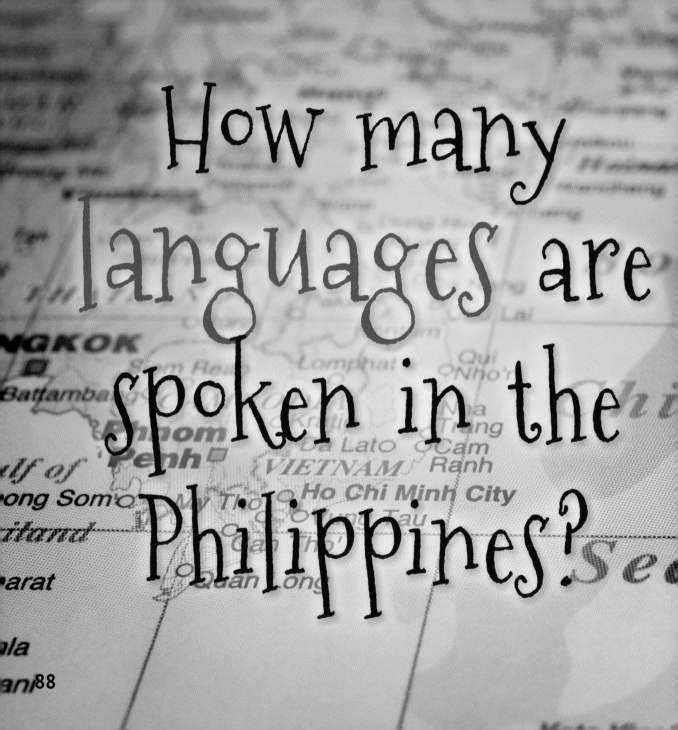

How many languages are spoken in the Philippines?

At least 72.

Think that's an oddly specific number? The Philippines has two official languages: Filipino and English. Filipino is a variation of Tagalog, the language of the people in the area around the capital, Manila. About 70 native languages are also spoken in the Philippines.

Why is Australia often referred to as being "down under"?

Because it lies entirely within the Southern Hemisphere.

Does that mean we should refer to countries entirely within the Northern Hemisphere as "up over"?

equator

Northern
Hemisphere

Southern
Hemisphere

World Book, Inc.
180 North LaSalle Street
Suite 900
Chicago, Illinois 60601
USA

For information about other "Answer Me This, World Book" titles, as well as other World Book print and digital publications, please go to www.worldbook.com.

For information about other World Book publications, call 1-800-WORLDBK (967-5325).

For information about sales to schools and libraries, call 1-800-975-3250 (United States) or 1-800-837-5365 (Canada).

Library of Congress Cataloging-in-Publication Data for this volume has been applied for.

Answer Me This, World Book
ISBN: 978-0-7166-3821-6 (set, hc.)

Why is Australia often referred to as being "down under"?
World Book answers your questions about people and places
ISBN: 978-0-7166-3828-5 (hc.)

Also available as:
ISBN: 978-0-7166-3838-4 (e-book)

Printed in China by RR Donnelley,
Guangdong Province
1st printing July 2019

Acknowledgments

Cover © David F, Getty Images; © Vitezslav Valka, Shutterstock
3-7   © Shutterstock
8-9   Library of Congress; © AM Stock Photo/Shutterstock; © Mahathir Mohd Yasin, Shutterstock
10-11 © AM Stock Photo/Shutterstock; © Mahathir Mohd Yasin, Shutterstock; © Corbis Historical/Getty Images
12-27 © Shutterstock
28-29 © Milan M, Shutterstock; © Corbis Historical/Getty Images
30-31 © Shutterstock
32-35 WORLD BOOK map
36-61 © Shutterstock
62-63 © Stefano Bianchetti, Getty Images
64-95 © Shutterstock

Staff

Editorial

Writers
Madeline King
Grace Guibert

Manager, New Content Development
Jeff De La Rosa

Manager, New Product Development
Nick Kilzer

Proofreader
Nathalie Strassheim

Manager, Contracts and Compliance
(Rights and Permissions)
Loranne K. Shields

Manager, Indexing Services
David Pofelski

Digital

Director, Digital Product
Development
Erika Meller

Digital Product Manager
Jonathan Wills

Graphics and Design

Senior Visual
Communications Designer
Melanie Bender

Media Editor
Rosalia Bledsoe

Manufacturing/Production

Manufacturing Manager
Anne Fritzinger

Production Specialist
Curley Hunter